THE WORLD'S SMALLEST COUNTRY and Other Geography Records

by Melissa Abramovitz

Consulting Editor: Gail Saunders-Smith, PhD

CAPSTONE PRESS
a capstone imprint

Pebble Plus is published by Capstone Press,
1710 Roe Crest Drive, North Mankato, Minnesota 56003
www.capstonepub.com

Copyright © 2014 by Capstone Press, a Capstone imprint. All rights reserved. No part of this publication may be reproduced in whole or in part, or stored in a retrieval system, or transmitted in any form or by any means, electronic, mechanical, photocopying, recording, or otherwise, without written permission of the publisher.

Library of Congress Cataloging-in-Publication Data
Abramovitz, Melissa, 1954–
  The world's smallest country and other geography records / by Melissa Abramovitz.
    pages cm.—(Pebble plus. wow!)
  Includes bibliographical references and index.
  Summary: "Simple text and colorful photos present record-breaking facts featuring geography topics"—Provided by publisher.
  ISBN 978-1-4765-0241-0 (library binding)
  ISBN 978-1-4765-3473-2 (ebook pdf)
  1. Geography—Miscellanea—Juvenile literature. I. Title.
  G133.A3 2104
  910—dc23   2013001987

Editorial Credits
Erika L. Shores, editor; Lori Bye, designer; Svetlana Zhurkin, media researcher; Jennifer Walker, production specialist

Photo Credits
Corbis: Nik Wheeler, 9; Newscom: Danita Delimont Photography/Bernard Friel, 15, WENN/ZOB/CB2, 5, World History Archive, 7; Shutterstock: Anastasios71, 17, Banauke, 13, Evgeni Stefanov, 21, Matteo Volpone, cover, Patryk Kosmider, 19, Redshinestudio (grunge border), throughout, TonyV3112, 11

Note to Parents and Teachers

The Wow! set supports national social studies standards related to people, places, and environments. This book describes and illustrates records relating to geography. The images support early readers in understanding the text. The repetition of words and phrases helps early readers learn new words. This book also introduces early readers to subject-specific vocabulary words, which are defined in the Glossary section. Early readers may need assistance to read some words and to use the Table of Contents, Glossary, Read More, Internet Sites, and Index sections of the book.

Printed in the United States of America in North Mankato, Minnesota.
032013   007223CGF13

TABLE OF CONTENTS

Cool Maps. 4
Cool Cities and Countries 8
Cool World Landmarks 16

Glossary 22
Read More 23
Internet Sites. 23
Index 24

COOL MAPS

Scientists created the tiniest map of the world. It's half as wide as a human hair. Ready for more cool geography facts?

5

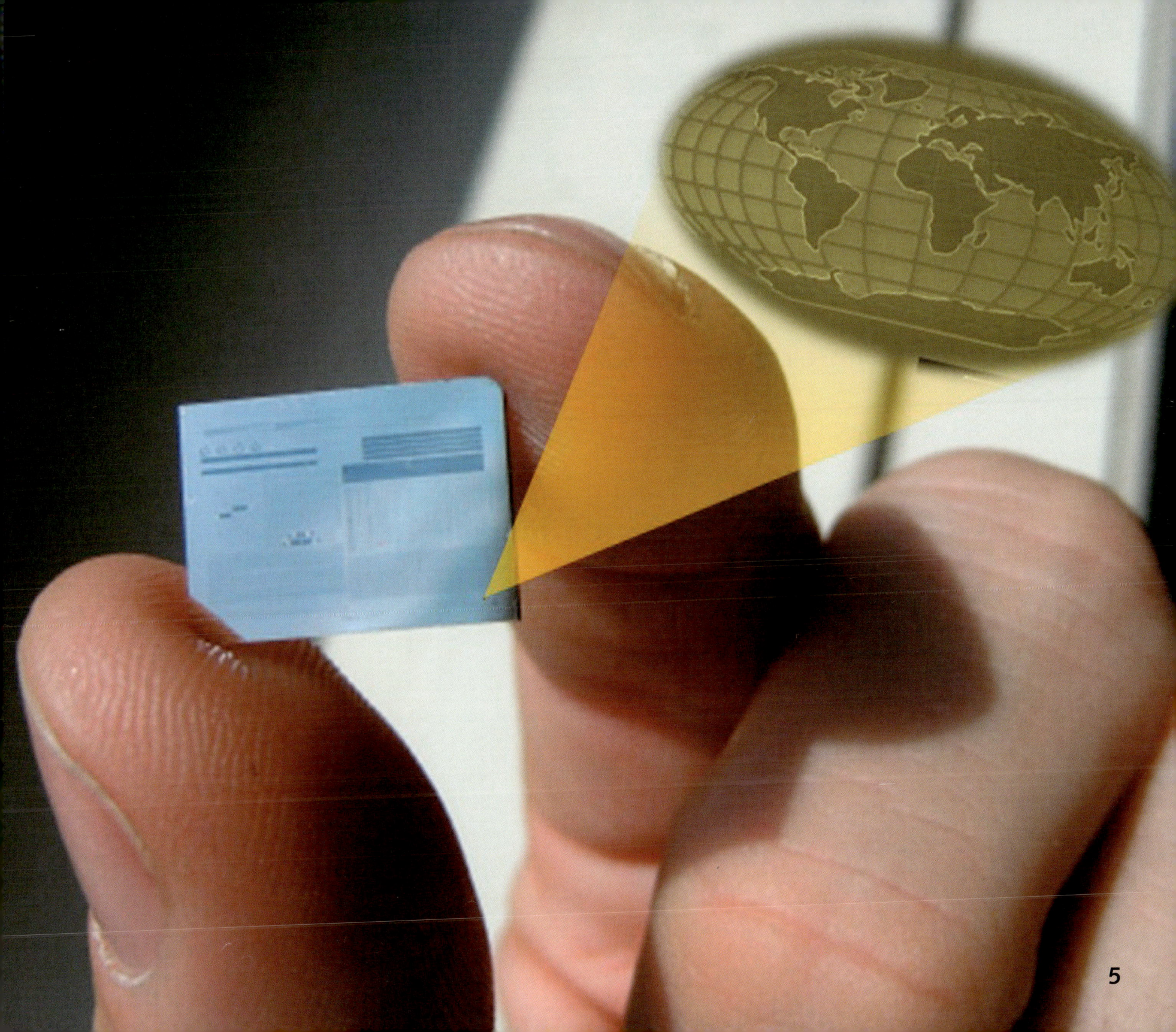

The world's oldest known map was carved in clay 4,000 years ago. It shows places in what is now Iraq.

7

COOL CITIES AND COUNTRIES

The world's first city was built 5,000 years ago. Uruk was home to as many as 80,000 people. Today only underground ruins are left in Iraq.

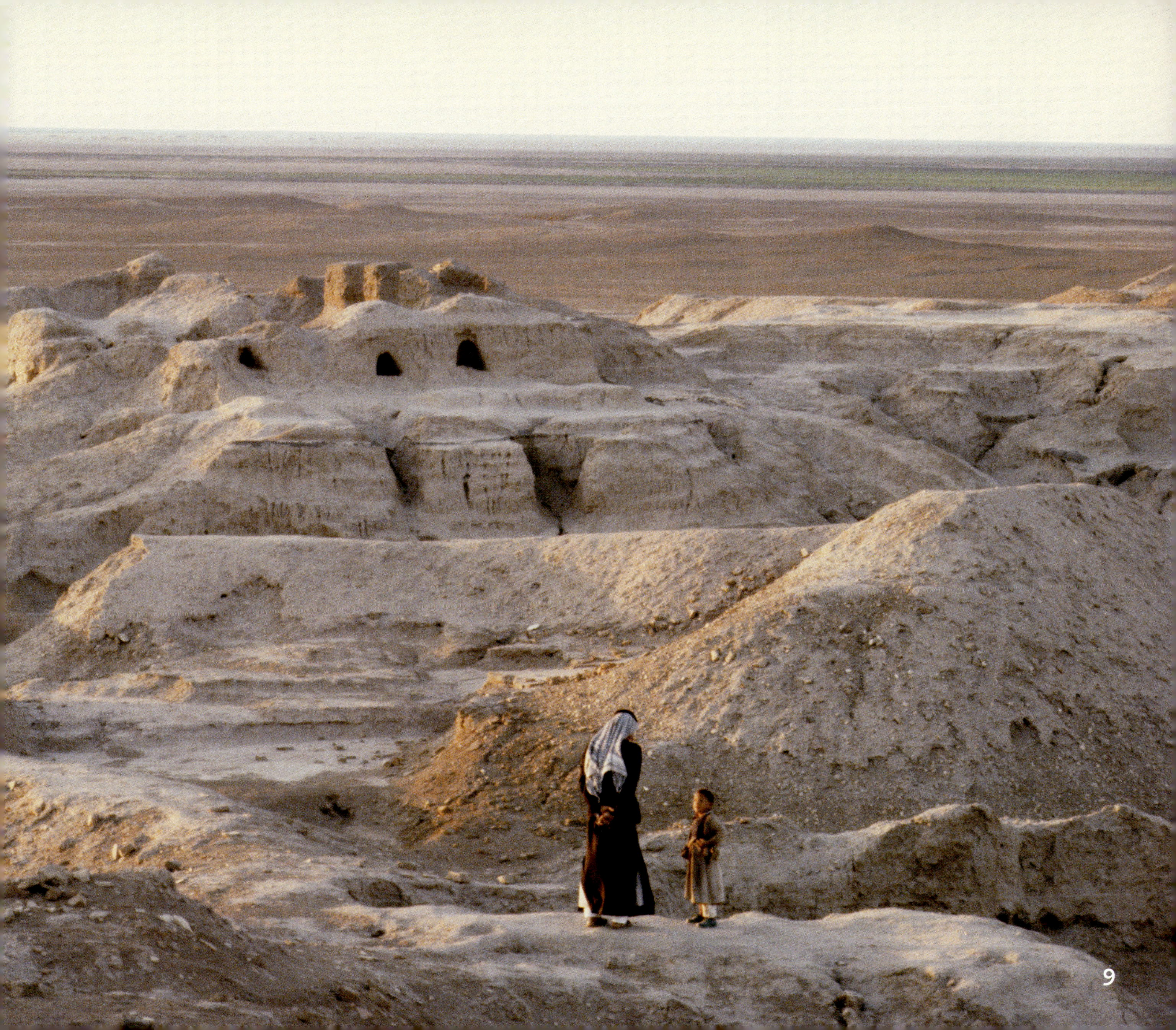

More people live in China than in any other country. China's population is 1.34 billion. The world's population is about 7 billion.

11

Vatican City is the smallest country. About 800 people live in a country not much bigger than Disneyland. Vatican City covers 109 acres (44 hectares).

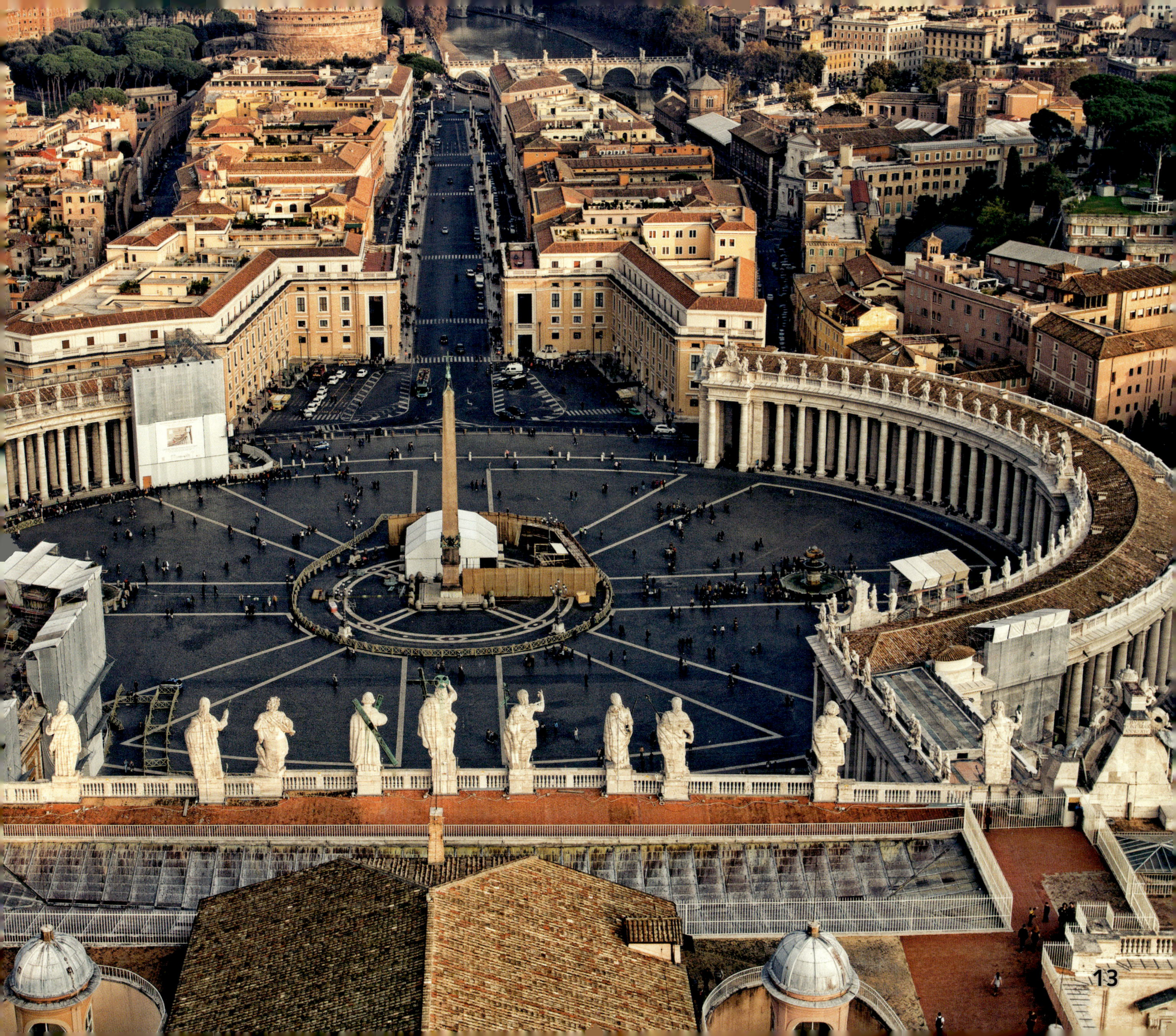

Papua New Guinea holds the record for the most languages spoken in a country. As many as 860 different languages are spoken there.

15

COOL WORLD LANDMARKS

Most skyscrapers stand less than 100 stories tall. The world's tallest building is Burj Khalifa in Dubai, United Arab Emirates. It has 160 stories.

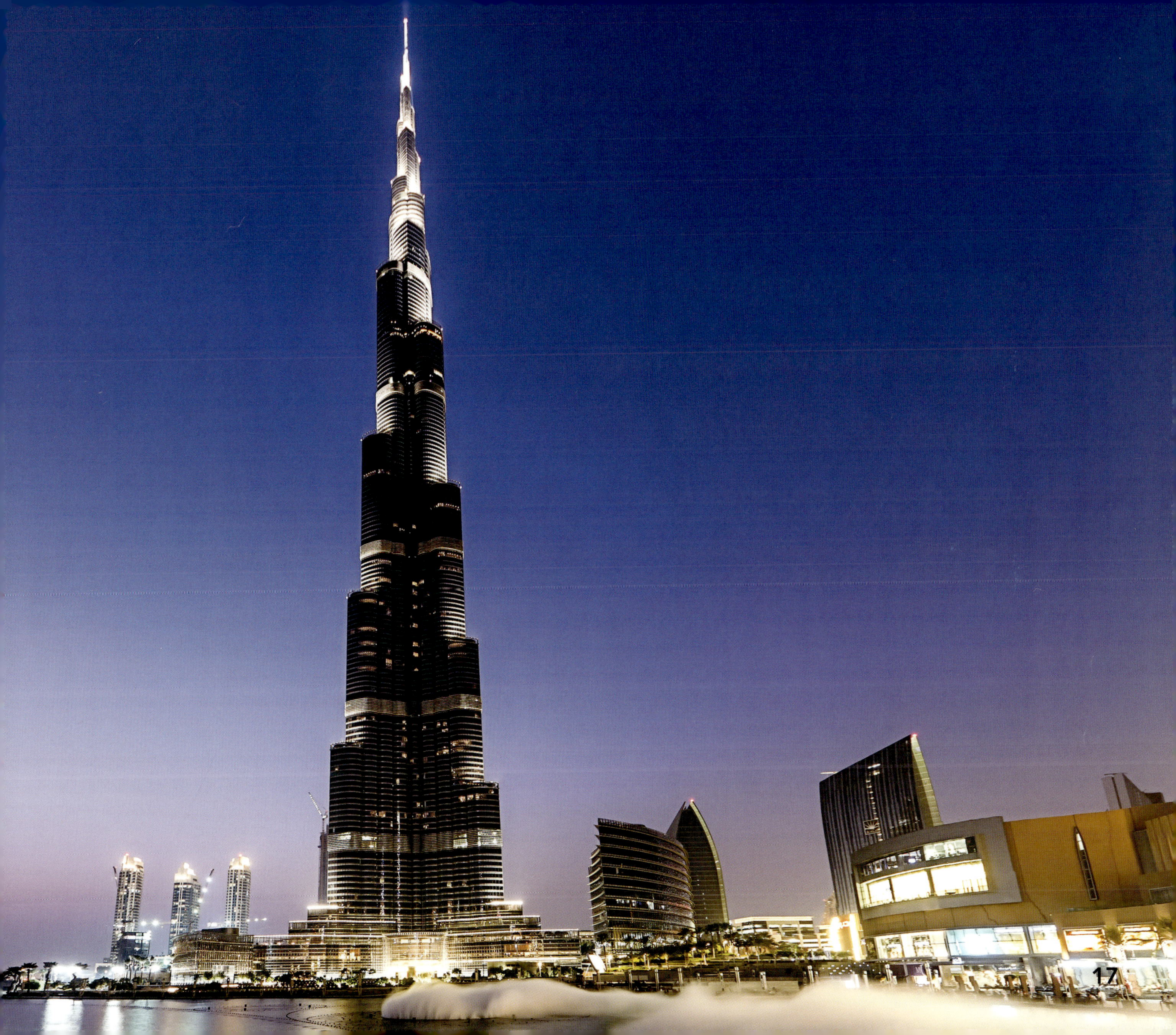

The Great Pyramid of Giza in Egypt is the world's tallest pyramid. It's made of 2.3 million stone blocks. It's 450 feet (137 meters) tall.

19

China's Great Wall is the biggest structure ever built. It took more than 2,000 years to build. Only parts of the 13,171-mile (21,197-kilometer) long wall still stand today.

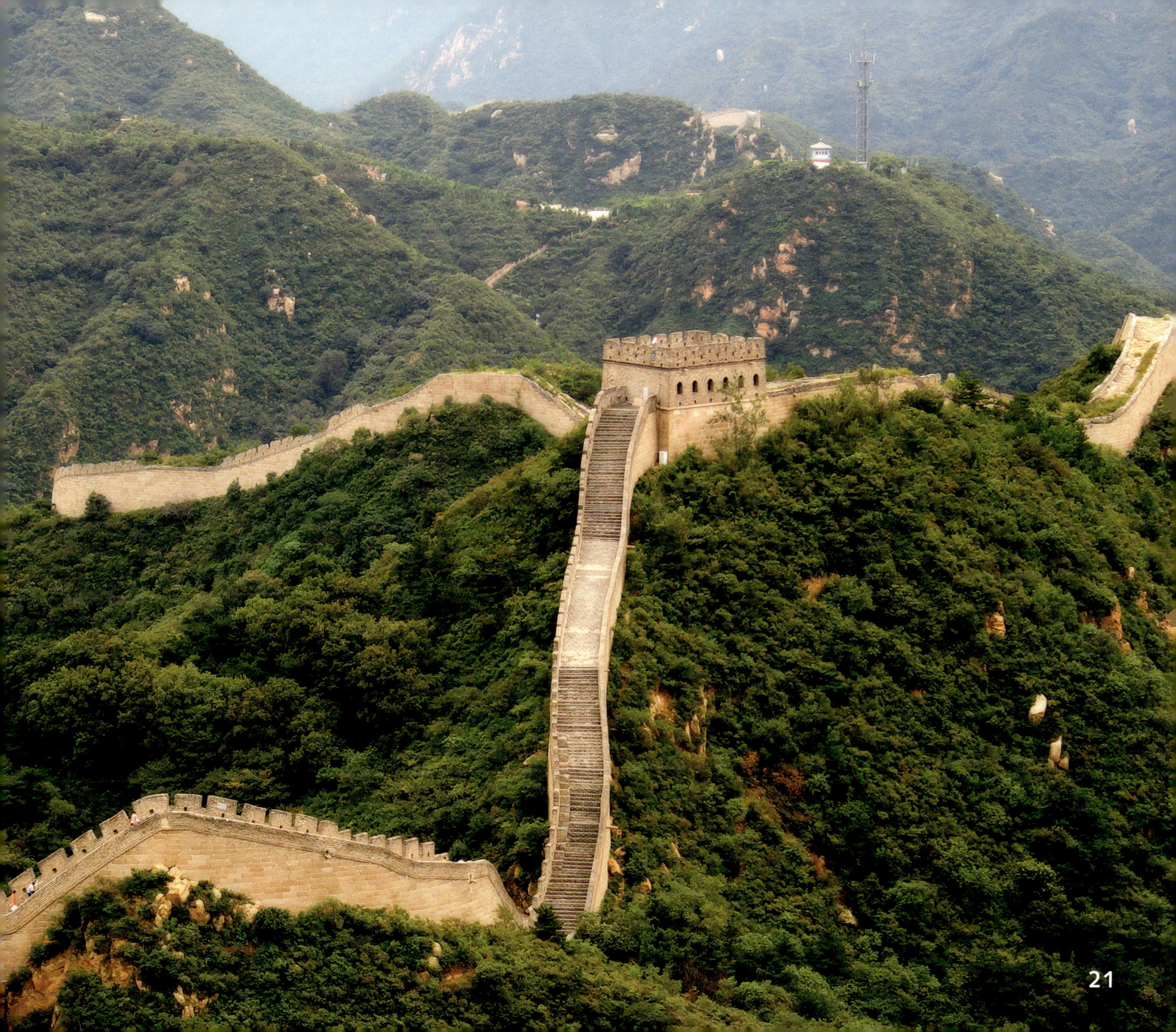

GLOSSARY

carve—to cut a shape out of a piece of stone, wood, or other material

geography—the study of places and the people that live there

population—how many people live in a particular place

pyramid—a triangle-shaped structure

record—when something is done better than anyone has ever done it before

ruins—the broken remains of ancient places

skyscraper—a very tall building

story—a level of a building

READ MORE

Gilpin, Daniel. *Record-breaking Buildings.* Record Breakers. New York: PowerKids Press, 2012.

Greve, Megan. *Maps Are Flat, Globes Are Round.* Little World Geography. Vero Beach, Fla.: Rourke Pub., 2010.

Riggs, Kate. *Great Wall of China.* Places of Old. Mankato, Minn.: Creative Education, 2009.

INTERNET SITES

FactHound offers a safe, fun way to find Internet sites related to this book. All of the sites on FactHound have been researched by our staff.

Here's all you do:

Visit www.facthound.com

Type in this code: 9781476502410

Super-cool stuff! Check out projects, games and lots more at www.capstonekids.com

INDEX

biggest population, 10
Burj Khalifa, 16
China, 10, 20
Dubai, United Arab Emirates, 16
Egypt, 18
first city, 8
Great Wall, 20
Iraq, 6

most languages, 14
oldest map, 6
Papua New Guinea, 14
smallest country, 12
smallest map, 4
tallest building, 16
tallest pyramid, 18
Uruk, 8
Vatican City, 12

Word Count: 215
Grade: 1
Early-Intervention Level: 19

MAR 1 9 2014